A Note to Parents W9-ARW-711

DK READERS is a compelling program for beginning readers, designed in conjunction with leading literacy experts, inclduing Dr. Linda Gambrell, Distinguished Professor of Education at Clemson University. Dr. Gambrell has served as President of the International Reading Association, National Reading Conference, and College Reading Association.

Beautiful illustrations and superb full-color photographs combine with engaging, easy-to-read stories to offer a fresh approach to each subject in the series. Each DK READER is guaranteed to capture a child's interest while developing his or her reading skills, general knowledge, and love of reading.

The five levels of DK READERS are aimed at different reading abilities, enabling you to choose the books that are exactly right for your child:

Pre-level 1: Learning to read
Level 1: Beginning to read
Level 2: Beginning to read alone
Level 3: Reading alone
Level 4: Proficient readers

The "normal" age at which a child begins to read can be anywhere from three to eight years old. Adult participation through the lower levels is very helpful for providing encouragement, discussing storylines, and sounding out unfamiliar words.

No matter which level you select, you can be sure that you are helping your child learn to read, then read to learn!

LONDON, NEW YORK, MUNICH,
MELBOURNE, AND DELHI

Editor Vicki Taylor
Designer Jill Clark
Managing Editor Catherine Saunders
Art Director Lisa Lanzarini
Publishing Manaer Simon Beecroft
Category Publisher Alex Allan
Production Editor Siu Chan
Production Controller Nick Seston

For Lucasfilm
Executive Editor Jonathan W. Rinzler
Art Director Troy Alders
Keeper of the Holocron Leland Chee
Director of Publishing Carol Roeder

Reading Consultant
Linda B. Gambrell, Ph.D.

First American Edition, 2010
10 11 10 9 8 7 6 5 4 3 2
Published in the United States by DK Publishing
375 Hudson Street, New York, New York 10014

DK books are available at special discounts when purchased in bulk
for sales promotions, premiums, fund-raising, or educational use.
For details, contact:
DK Publishing Special Markets
375 Hudson Street
New York, New York 10014
SpecialSales@dk.com

A catalog record for this book is available
from the Library of Congress.

ISBN: 978-0-7566-6314-8 (Paperback)
ISBN: 978-0-7566-6315-5 (Hardcover)

Color reproduction by Media Development Printing Ltd, UK.
Printed and bound in China by L Rex Printing Co., Ltd.

Discover more at
www.dk.com

www.starwars.com

Contents

DK READERS

READING
3
ALONE

STAR WARS
Death Star Battles

Written by Simon Beecroft

DK Publishing

LUCAS BOOKS

That's no moon!

You are flying through
deep space.
Suddenly a small
enemy fighter ship
shoots past.
Where did it
come from?
All you can see
is a small moon
up ahead.
Wait, that's no moon.
It is too big.
Quick, turn back!
Something is wrong with your ship.
It will not turn around!
You are being pulled toward the
most deadly battle station in the
galaxy: the Death Star.

The Death Star is the evil Empire's
ultimate weapon. It has a superlaser
that is powerful enough to destroy an
entire planet with one gigantic blast.

The Death Star
The Death Star
has a population of
about 1.7 million
people and over
400,000 droids.

How to build a Death Star

Only one man in the galaxy is evil
enough to need a planet-destroying
superweapon: Emperor Palpatine.
The Emperor is a vile Sith Lord.
He rules the galaxy alongside Darth
Vader and huge armies of deadly
stormtroopers. The Emperor will do
anything he can to increase
his power.
He plans to use the
Death Star to destroy
his enemies and the
Rebel Alliance.

Tarkin oversees construction of the Death Star with the Emperor and Darth Vader

Grand Moff Tarkin is one of the Emperor's top commanders. He masterminded the construction of the Death Star for Emperor Palpatine. He used a clever species of engineers, the Geonosians and he forced many Wookiee slaves and other prisoners to build the fearsome weapon.

Conference room

Grand Moff Tarkin and Darth Vader command the Death Star from the overbridge, where they make their sinister plans in a dark room in the overbridge. The Death Star has a special trained fighting force; Death Star Troopers.

Two Death Star Troopers stand guard during top-level meetings. The Imperial leaders sit around a black table with a holoprojector in the middle for displaying tactical holograms or maps. During meetings Darth Vader sometimes intimidates his officers by using the dark side of the Force.

Fire when ready…

Grand Moff Tarkin and Darth Vader have captured Princess Leia, an important Rebel leader. They want her to tell them the location of the Rebels' hidden base. They threaten to destroy her home planet Alderaan if she refuses. Leia says the base is on a planet called Dantooine. But then Tarkin decides to destroy Alderaan to show the Rebels what a powerful weapon the Empire has.

The disk-shaped superweapon blasts out eight beams of light that join together into one powerful laser beam. The small green planet is blown into space dust.

Superlaser
The Death Star's superlaser uses so much energy to fire that it takes 24 hours to recharge before it can be fired again.

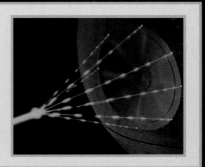

Trapped!

While Leia is being held prisoner on the Death Star, Luke Skywalker is on his way to Alderaan. He is traveling in a starship called the *Millennium Falcon*. With him are Jedi Knight Obi-Wan Kenobi, captain Han Solo, a Wookiee named Chewbacca, and two droids C-3PO and R2-D2.

When they arrive where Alderaan used to be, they see a TIE Fighter. It heads straight toward a small moon which turns out to be the Death Star.

The Death Star uses an invisible tractor beam to grab hold of Luke's ship so it cannot escape. They are pulled into a docking bay within a mile-high trench that runs around the middle of the Death Star.

Deadly surface

The surface of the Death Star is covered with weapons, including 10,000 turbolaser guns and 2,500 laser cannons. 8,000 tractor beam projectors can trap any enemy ships that come too close.

Into the Death Star

The *Falcon* is forced to land in a giant hangar. An invisible shield across the entrance maintains the artificial atmosphere.

Docking bays

The Death Star has many docking bays for spaceships. Some are designed for visiting ships, others are hangars for Imperial fighters such as TIE.

Beside the ship is a large hole in the floor, which has an elevator to raise and lower ships for repairs.

Control room windows overlook the hangar. They are surrounded by stormtroopers.

Stormtroopers

Stormtroopers are the Empire's elite soldiers. They wear white helmets that cover their faces and suits of armor made up of 18 pieces.

Stormtroopers are armed with blaster pistols or blaster rifles.

A squad of stormtroopers boards the *Falcon*. They are looking for the crew. Luke and the others are hiding in secret compartments beneath the floor.

Tour of duty
At least 25,000 stormtroopers serve on the Death Star at any one time. They patrol every part of the enormous battle station.

I can't see in this helmet!

Han and Luke ambush two
stormtroopers and steal their armor.
Disguised as stormtroopers, they
discover that Princess Leia is a prisoner.

Turbolifts

Elevators, called turbolifts, connect all sectors of the Death Star. Turbolifts move up and down as well as side to side. Some turbolifts are reserved for officers.

Luke has a plan to rescue her.

They handcuff Chewbacca so they can pretend he is their prisoner.

Han and Luke try to look relaxed in their stormtrooper disguises as they wait for a turbolift to arrive.

Troops, bureaucrats, and robots move about, but most of them ignore the trio. Only a few glance at the giant Wookiee.

Prison break

Finally, Luke and Han find the prison
block in which Leia is being held.
But an Imperial officer becomes
suspicious and they have a blaster battle.
After Luke finds Leia, more stormtroopers
arrive, cutting off their only exit.
Han and Luke exchange fire with
the stormtroopers.

Interrogator droid
Imperial cell blocks are horrible places. Security cameras spy on prisoners while interrogator droids electroshock them to force them to answer questions.

Leia has to think very fast now.
The only way out is a garbage chute!

Something is alive in here!

Luke, Leia, Han, and Chewbacca whiz down the garbage chute and land in a smelly, dirty trash compactor. This is where garbage of every kind is collected before being crushed and dumped into space. It is totally sealed.

Dianoga serpent
Dianogas, or garbage squids, live in trash compactors, refuse pits and sewers across the galaxy, feeding on scraps and rubbish.

When Han tries to blast his way out,
the laserbolt bounces around the small
metal room and nearly hits one of them.
Then they hear a frightening growl and
realize something is living in there.
Suddenly, a long tentacle grabs hold of
Luke and pulls him underwater!
The others think Luke is gone forever,
but the creature spits him out.
Then the walls start closing in.
They are going to be crushed!

Droids to the rescue

Luke shouts into his comlink to get help from C-3PO and R2-D2.

But C-3PO cannot answer because stormtroopers are searching the control room.

The droid tells them that Luke and the others are heading for the prison block level. The stormtroopers go after Luke, Han, and Chewbacca.

C-3PO finally hears Luke begging the droids to turn off the garbage masher. The droids can hear them screaming. They think that their friends are being crushed to death. Actually, they are whooping for joy because the walls have stopped closing in. Well done, R2-D2!

Desperate leap

As Luke and Leia are
trying to escape the deadly
stormtroopers, they run
through a doorway—and
nearly fall from a ledge to
their death. Below them is a
deep shaft that appears to go
on forever!

Luke fires at the stormtroopers
and Leia hits a switch that
shuts the door, leaving them
perched on the short ledge.
But the stormtroopers are
opening the door.

On the other side of the chasm, more
stormtroopers begin to blast at them.
Luke fires at the new enemies, but then
he has an idea.

Air shafts

There are many air shafts throughout the Death Star. They are part of a system that allows fresh air to circulate through the interior.

He grabs a cable attached to his utility belt and throws it upward so it catches onto an overhanging pipe.
He scoops up Leia and they swing across to safety!

Solo Mission

Machines called reactor couplings power the huge tractor beam.
This is the beam that is preventing Han's ship from leaving the Death Star. Obi-Wan knows that if he switches off one of these machines, he will free the *Falcon*.

He slips past stormtroopers using the
Force to stay hidden.

Obi-Wan finally reaches the reactor
coupling. It stands on a shaft inside
a trench that seems to be a hundred
miles deep.

The Jedi edges his way along a narrow
ledge that leads to a control panel.
He quickly turns off the machines.

Final duel

The most fearsome presence on the Death Star is Darth Vader. His black caped figure walking down the corridor is a terrifying sight. Vader can sense that Obi-Wan Kenobi is on the Death Star and tracks him down. They confront each other. Swoosh! Their lightsabers clash and spark!

Lost friendship

Darth Vader is a Sith Lord who was once Jedi Knight Anakin. Anakin is Luke's father. Obi-Wan was Anakin's Master until Anakin became a Sith. Anakin fought Obi-Wan, but lost. He has wanted revenge since then.

Luke watches Obi-Wan block Vader's every move, until the old Jedi Master stands still with a calm look on his face. Vader strikes down Kenobi with a single slash of his blade. Obi-Wan's cloak falls to the floor, but he is not in it.

Luke cries out, "No!" as Vader prods the empty robe with his foot.

We are not safe yet!

Thanks to Obi-Wan, the *Falcon* blasts off from the deadly Death Star. But TIE fighters give chase. Luke and Han work together, manning their turbolasers and blowing up all the enemy ships.

Han and Luke are relieved, but Leia thinks Tarkin has let them escape. Leia is right—Tarkin is tracking their ship. He still wants to find out the location of the Rebels' hidden base.

X-Wings

X-wings are starfighters. They have four wings, called S-foils, which form the shape of an 'X'. They are made by a company called Incom.

Rebel attack

The Death Star is more powerful than half the entire firepower of the Imperial Starfleet. But the Rebels think they have found a way to destroy it.

Rebel pilots must use all their skill to fly

Rebel briefing
At the Rebel base on Yavin 4, the Rebels study the Death Star plans that R2-D2 has been carrying. Leia knows that the Rebels must act fast if they want to outsmart Vader.

along a narrow tunnel on the surface of
the Death Star.

At the end of the tunnel is an exhaust
port. If they can fire a laser bolt right
into this tiny hole, the bolt will
penetrate the main reactor.

This will start a chain reaction that
should destroy the station.

The Rebels hope that their ships are
small enough to avoid the Death Star's
outer defences, which are designed to
stop large-scale assaults.

Turbolaser defense

The Death Star has powerful turbolasers, but the starfighters are nimble. The Death Star's defenses are also not strong enough against the Force.

When Obi-Wan tells Luke to "use the Force" instead of his targeting computer, Luke fires two proton torpedos into the Reactor Core.

The battle station is destroyed before
it can attack the Rebel base.
But the sinister Emperor will not let this
stop him. He has a plan...

The second Death Star

After the destruction of the Death Star at the Battle of Yavin, Emperor Palpatine orders the construction of a second Death Star. This battle station is even larger than the first, with thousands more turbolasers. The second Death Star also has a planet-destroying superlaser—but it can be recharged in only three minutes. This superlaser can also fire at small targets, such as enemy ships. It is more powerful and accurate.

The Emperor is sure that, this time, he will crush forever the Rebel rebellion.

Emperor Palpatine arrives

The Emperor's personal shuttle lands on the new Death Star. He has arrived to inspect the new battle station.

He is greeted by Darth Vader.
Hundreds of stormtroopers line
up and the Imperial Red Guards
bow to him.
The Emperor wants this Death
Star to look unfinished in order to
trick the Rebels into attacking.
In fact, its superlaser is already a
dangerous weapon!
When the Rebels attack, the
Emperor intends to destroy their
fleet once and for all!

The throne room

Emperor Palpatine has a private command center on the second Death Star. It is located on top of a 100-storey tower on the North Pole of the superweapon.

Security is very high around the throne room to stop any intruders.

Each entrance has a trap and is guarded by the Emperor's Imperial Guards.

There is a docking rig for the Emperor's personal shuttle and a sleep chamber that monitors his health.

Emperor Palpatine sits on a large throne. From there he contemplates his most horrible plan—to turn Luke to the dark side! He is sure that Luke will kill Vader, Luke's father, and therefore become a Sith Lord and the Emperor's new apprentice.

Final battle

The Rebels decide to attack the second
Death Star because it seems weak and
unprotected, just as the Emperor
planned. The Rebel fleet is led by Han's

friend Lando Calrissian, who is flying the *Falcon*. They don't know it is a trap. Meanwhile, Palpatine tricks Luke into battle with Darth Vader. Luke defeats his father—but refuses to kill him. So, the Emperor unleashes unstoppable Sith lightning at Luke. At the last moment, Darth hurls the Emperor into an abyss, saving Luke's life.

Most powerful Jedi
Because Luke feels compassion for his father, Darth Vader, he reveals himself to be the most powerful Jedi of them all.

Battle of Endor

A Rebel team, led by Han Solo and
Princess Leia, destroys the shield
generator protecting the Death Star.
This allows the *Falcon* to fly into its
interior, chased by TIE fighters.

Lando and his friends blast away at the main reactor.
The Death Star explodes!
Emperor Palpatine is dead.
All over the galaxy, people celebrate their new freedom.

Big explosion
The second Death Star becomes a ball of flames and the *Falcon* flies away. The Rebels have won!

Glossary

Ambush
A surprise attack made by people from a hiding place.

Armor
Protective clothing.

Artificial
Fake or not real.

Bureaucrat
An office worker.

Chain Reaction
An event that leads to another important event happening.

Engineer
A person who designs and makes machinery or vehicles.

Enormous
Unusually big.

Fearsome
Very frightening.

The Force
A mysterious energy that can be used for good or evil.

Geonosian
Insectoid race from the planet Geonosis.

Hangar
A large, warehouse building or room for housing spaceships or vehicles.

Holoprojector
A device that projects a hologram.

Nimble
Fast and able to change direction quickly.

Reactor Coupling
The system that powers the tractor beams.

Sinister
Very bad, mysterious, and scary.

Sith Lord
A leader of the evil Siths who use the dark side of the Force.

Slave
Someone who is owned by a master and is forced to do everything they are told to.

Stormtrooper
Members of the Emperor's personal army.

Tentacle
The long, flexible legs and arms of a creature with many limbs.

Terrifying
Extremely scary and frightening.

Tractor Beam
A beam that can pull one object toward another.